My name is

_____

and this is my book.

If lost, please return it to me.

Thank you.

GOD MADE ME, THE EARTH, AND THE SEA

COLORING & ACTIVITY BOOK

YOLANDA N. BRANNON, PSY.D.

ISBN-13: 978-0615866697
ISBN-10: 0615866697

Printed in U.S.A.

This book is dedicated

to

the children of all nations.

Acknowledgements

All honor is given to God; the Father, Son, and Holy Ghost. He gave the inspiration for the words and illustrations of this book. Thank you to those who continue to support this ministry and its efforts to spread the gospel throughout all nations. Thank you to my family and friends for their continued unwavering love and support.

God made me, the earth, and the sea.
Come along this journey and see.

In the beginning the earth was empty, dark, and filled with water.

God looked at it and wondered, "What can I add to it?"

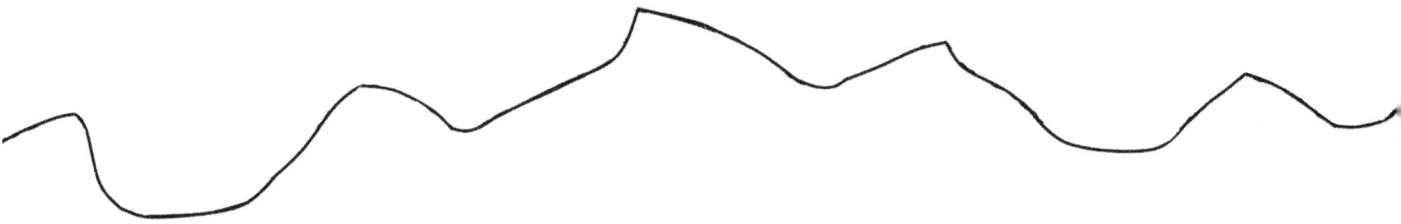

Below is a hidden bible verse. Look carefully at the chart below. Each alphabet matches a number. Match the alphabet with the number to complete the secret code below.

For example, "A = 1" and "B = 2"

A	B	C	D	E	F	G	H	I	J	K	L	M
1	2	3	4	5	6	7	8	9	10	11	12	13

N	O	P	Q	R	S	T	U	V	W	X	Y	Z
14	15	16	17	18	19	20	21	22	23	24	25	26

I __   __ __ __   b __ __ __ n n __ __ __
9 14   20 8 5   2 5 7 9 14 14 9 14 7

G __ __   __ __ __ __ t __ d   __ __ __
7 15 4   3 18 5 1 20 5 4   20 8 5

__ __ __ v __ __ s   __ __ __   __ __ __
8 5 1 22 5 14 19   1 14 4   20 8 5

__ a __ __ __.
5 1 18 20 8

Genesis 1:1 (NIV)

Light of Day

On the 1st day
he made light.
God looked at it
and smiled.

Night

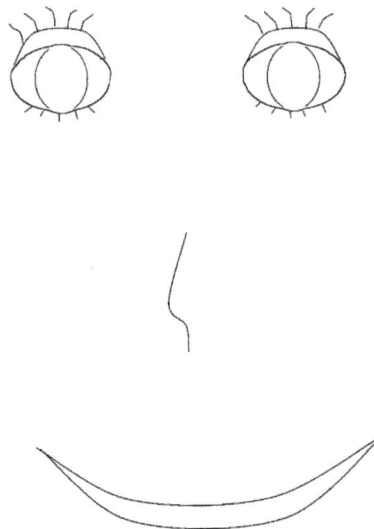

He liked the light
for day. He kept
the darkness
for night.

The light of day

is for bright

sunny days

and. . . .

o help plants grow and for playing outdoors.

13

The "Light of Day" allows us to do a lot of things.
Write 3 of your favorite day time activities below.

My Favorite Day Time Activities

1. _____

2. _____

3. _____

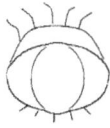

The darkness of

night lets us

know when it's

time to.....

PLAY ROOM

CARS | AIR PLANES | BOARD GAMES
TRUCKS | SOLDIERS | BALLS
MORCYLES | TRAIN | BLOCKS

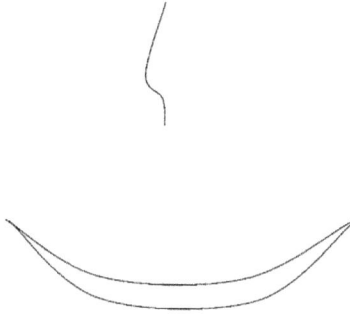

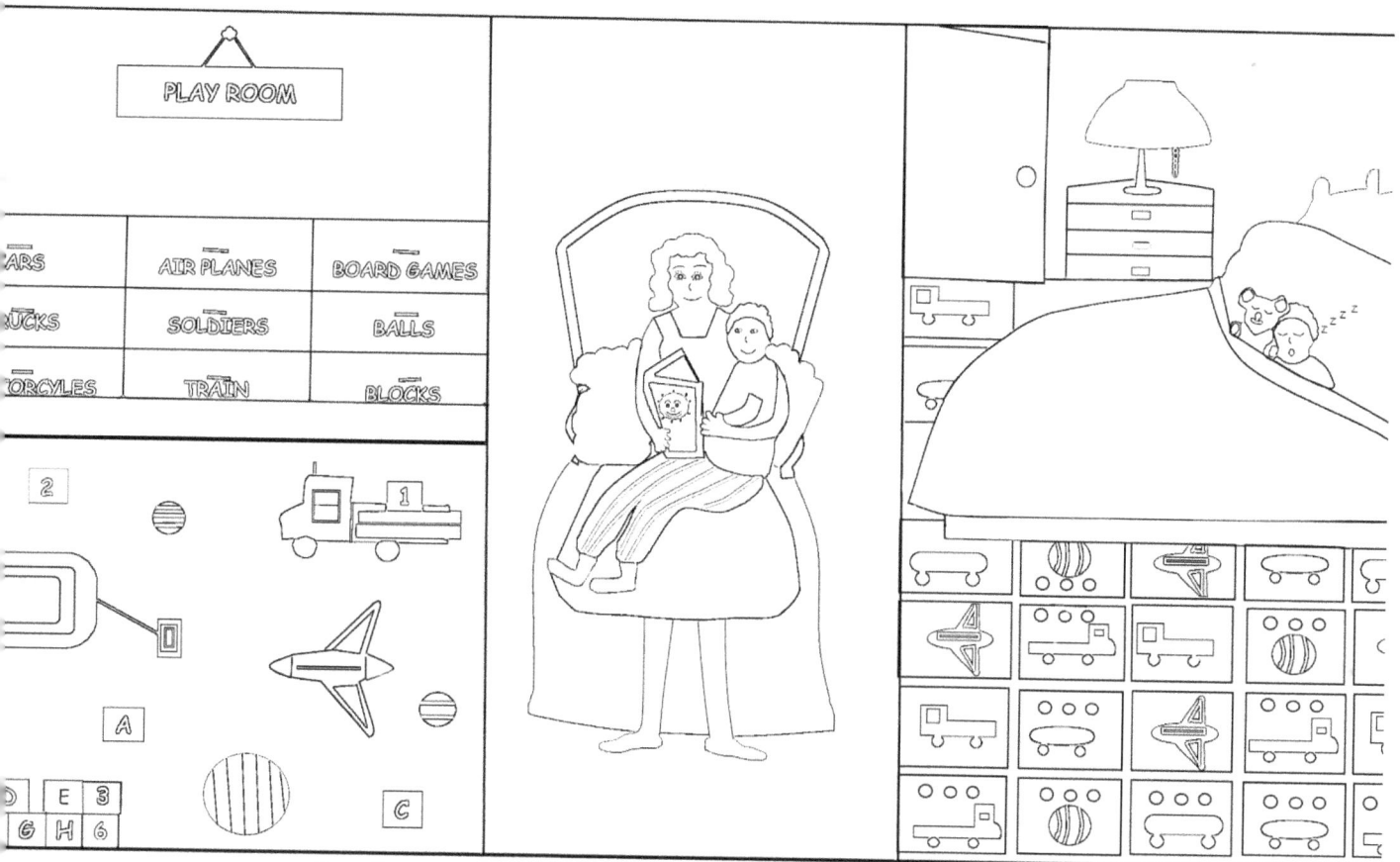

put toys away, read a story,
and say "good night."

Instructions

Write 3 of your favorite bedtime or night time activities below.

My Favorite Bedtime/Night Activities

1. _____

2. _____

3. _____

On the 2nd day, the earth was still filled with water. God made a vault called "sky" to separate the water.

He put water above the sky and beneath the sky. The water above the sky gives us rain, sleet, and snow.

He named sky the "heavens."

On the 3rd day, God played with the water. He divided the water into shallow rivers and streams.

He kept some of the water very deep and called it the "sea."

"I love to drink water. It cools me off."

POOL RULES
1. Life guard always on duty.
2. Swim safely.

CLEAN TOWELS

USED TOWELS

8FT   5FT   3FT

8FT   5FT   3FT

WATER

BUBBLES

"It's fu

"I love bath time."

We use water to drink, swim, and bathe.

Instructions

Draw a picture in the box below of you enjoying the water on God's earth.

On the 3rd day, God made the land.

Orange Tree

Apple Tree

The land is where fruits, vegetables, trees, and grass grows.

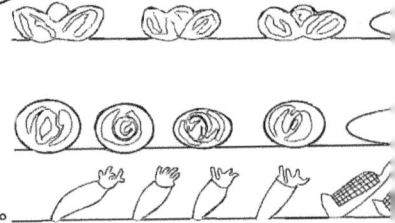

The land gives us lots of sand to build castles along the shore.

20

Instructions

The land (soil, dirt, or sand) is used for many things. Fruits, vegetables, and flowers are grown from the soil. Write 3 of your favorite fruits and vegetables below.

My Favorite Fruits and Vegetables

1. _____

2. _____

3. _____

Activity 1
Grow a Flower in a Special Pot

Materials Needed:
-1 small or medium pot with drainage holes underneath
-Some potting soil (amount varies depending on the size of the pot)
-1 packet of seeds (your choice)
-Water
-Sunlight

Instructions:
<u>Step 1</u>: Read about the flower. It is good to know how to take care of it and how much water and sunlight it needs.
<u>Step 2</u>: Fill your special pot about three-quarters with potting soil. We will call this soil, "the bottom layer" of soil.
<u>Step 3</u>: Read the directions on the packet. Open the packet of seeds and sprinkle them in the pot over the "bottom layer" of potting soil. Put a thin "top layer" of soil over the seeds. Don't put too much soil. Don't smash the soil in the pot.
<u>Step 4</u>: Water your new plant and place it in an area outdoors or indoors where it can get some sunlight. Be sure to water your plant throughout the week.

Activity 2
Share a Seed with Someone

God's holy word can be a seed in the life of another boy or girl even an adult. Did you know that you can plant and water a seed in the life of someone? Share the word of God with someone daily.

Materials Needed:
-Bible verse, information, and knowledge about God (e.g., God loves you)

Instructions:
Tell a friend, neighbor, family member, and everyone about the Lord our God.

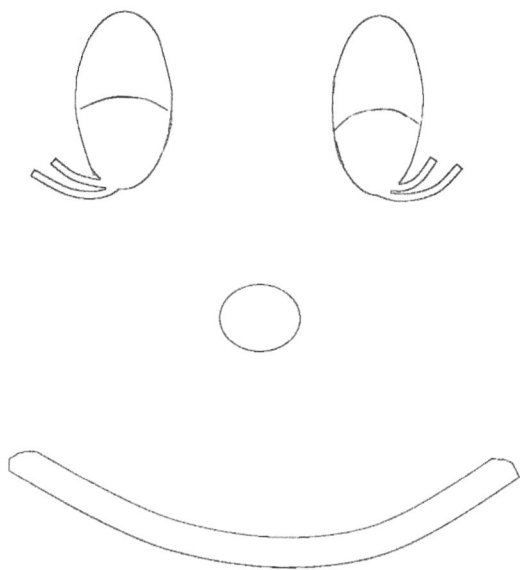

On day 4, God looked at the light of day and the darkness of night.

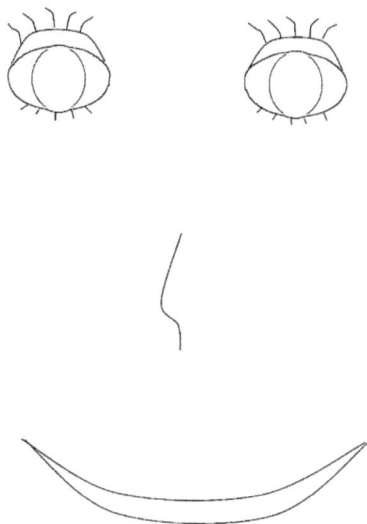

"Hum, something is missing," said God.

God liked the light of day.

He liked the darkness of night.

So he hung them both in the

vault he called "sky."

God decided to decorate
the light of day and the
darkness of night.

He formed the sun, moon, stars,
planets, all the seasons of the
year.

25

Instructions

Below is a secret code. Look carefully at the chart below. Each alphabet matches a number. Match the alphabet with the number to complete the secret code below.

For example, "A = 1" and "B = 2"

A	B	C	D	E	F	G	H	I	J	K	L	M
1	2	3	4	5	6	7	8	9	10	11	12	13

N	O	P	Q	R	S	T	U	V	W	X	Y	Z
14	15	16	17	18	19	20	21	22	23	24	25	26

The rainbow was created by God and is a symbol of ....

a __   __ t __ __ __ __ __   __ p __ __ __ __ __ __   __ __ __ __ __ __ __
1 14   5 20 5 18 14 1 12   16 18 15 13 9 19 5   2 5 20 23 5 5 14

G __ __   __ __ __   __ __ __   __ i __ __ __ __   __ __ __ __ __ __ r __ __
7 15 4   1 14 4   1 12 12   12 9 22 9 14 7   3 18 5 1 20 21 18 5 19

__ __   __ v __ __ __   __ __ __ __   __ __   __ t __ __   __ __ __ __ __ __.
15 6   5 22 5 18 25   11 9 14 4   15 14   20 8 5   5 1 18 20 8

**Learn more about the true meaning of the rainbow by reading Genesis 9:8-16 in your bible.

Instructions

God decorated the light of day and the darkness of night.
Complete the word search puzzle.

x	c	k	a	u	s	p
v	l	a	b	v	r	l
m	o	o	n	x	a	a
b	u	w	t	f	t	n
p	d	d	w	s	s	e
i	s	a	b	j	y	t
s	g	s	u	n	g	s

planets sun moon	stars clouds

Instructions

God decorated the sky and called it the "heavens." He also gave us changes in the weather. Complete the crossword puzzle below to learn more about God's creation.

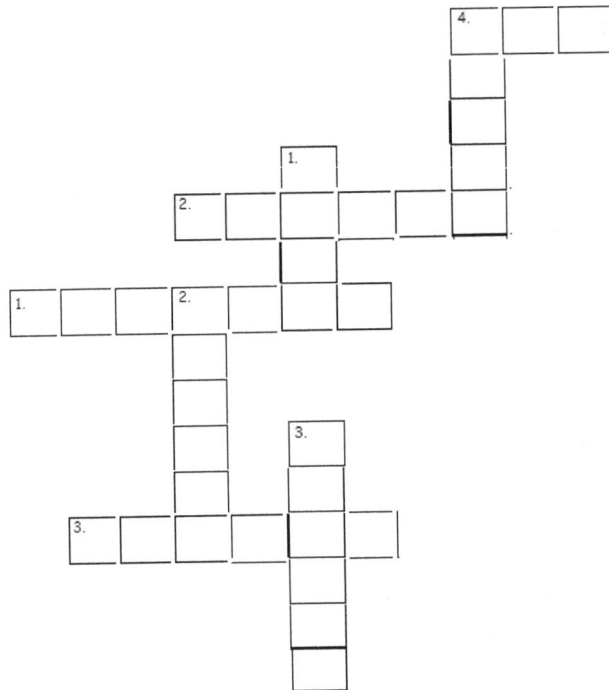

Across

1) What are Spring, summer, Autumn (fall), and winter?
2) This is found in the sky. It is white and appears "fluffy."
3) The time (season) of year when flowers bloom and April showers water the earth.
4) This is found in the sky and gives us bright sunny days.

Down-Up

1) Found in the sky. Gives light at night and changes (full, half, etc).
2) The time (season) of year when school is out and it is very hot.
3) The time (season) of year when it is cold and there may be snow and ice on the ground.
4) Found in the sky, seen at night, small in size, and too many to count.

28

On the 5th day, God made the creatures that play and live in the sea.

He made fish, whales, dolphins, sharks, and every living creature of the sea.

He even made birds to fly over the sea to hum sweet melodies.

"Hello."

"Good to see you."

"Lots of traffic today."

"Excuse me."

"Feels good."

"Good Morning."

"Sure."

29

Instructions

God made all the creatures of the sea. Complete the word search puzzle.

```
j  e  l  l  y  f  i  s  h
o  c  t  o  p  u  s  h  s
w  r  u  j  w  r  q  a  i
h  a  r  w  w  n  u  r  f
a  b  t  z  e  o  i  k  d
l  d  l  e  f  m  d  v  l
e  i  e  e  l  u  i  z  o
d  o  l  p  h  i  n  h  g
c  r  o  c  o  d  i  l  e
```

whale	dolphin	gold fish
shark	octopus	jelly fish
crab	squid	crocodile
eel	turtle	

On the 6th day, God made the animals that live and play on the land.

He made giraffes, elephants, lions, cows, horses, and bears.

He made every living creature on the land.

31

Instructions

God made all the animals on the land. Complete the word search puzzle.

```
h   o   r   s   e   c   a   t
e   l   e   p   h   a   n   t
g   i   r   a   f   f   e   i
t   n   o   i   l   n   j   g
z   e   b   r   a   e   a   e
m   f   o   x   b   e   a   r
p   c   o   w   n   d   o   g
m   o   n   k   e   y   x   m
```

Horse	Tiger	Elephant
Cow	Bear	Giraffe
Lion	Fox	Monkey
Zebra	Dog	Cat

God looked at the creatures of the sea
and the animals on the land and wondered,
"Who can I put on earth to name them and
take care of them?"

"Hello"

"Hi"

"It's a good day."

Instructions

Below is a hidden bible verse. Look carefully at the chart below. Each alphabet matches a number. Match the alphabet with the number to complete the secret code below.

For example, "A = 1" and "B = 2"

A	B	C	D	E	F	G	H	I	J	K	L	M
1	2	3	4	5	6	7	8	9	10	11	12	13

N	O	P	Q	R	S	T	U	V	W	X	Y	Z
14	15	16	17	18	19	20	21	22	23	24	25	26

S __   G __ __   __ __ __ __ t __ d
19 15   7 15 4   3 18 5 1 20 5 4

__ a __ k __ __ __   __ __   __ __ __
13 1 14 11 9 14 4   9 14   8 9 19

__ w __   __ m __ __ e,   __ __   __ __ __
15 23 14   9 13 1 7 5   9 14   20 8 5

__ m __ __ __   __ __   G __ __   h __
9 13 1 7 5   15 6   7 15 4   8 5

__ __ __ __ t __ d   __ h __ __;
3 18 5 1 20 5 4   20 8 5 13

m __ __ __   __ __ __   f __ __ __ __ __
13 1 12 5   1 14 4   6 5 13 1 12 5

h __   c __ __ __ t __ __   __ __ e __.
8 5   3 18 5 1 20 5 4   20 8 5 13

Genesis 1:27 (NIV)

34

God said, "I will make a man in my image from the dirt of the ground."
God blew the breath of life into the man's nose and he became alive.

God then said, "It is not good for the man to be alone. I will make a woman in my image for him. She will help the man take care of all that I created."

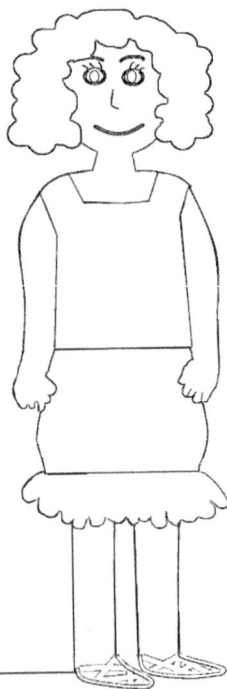

God told the man and woman to rule over the fish in the sea, the birds in the sky, the animals on the land, and every living thing.

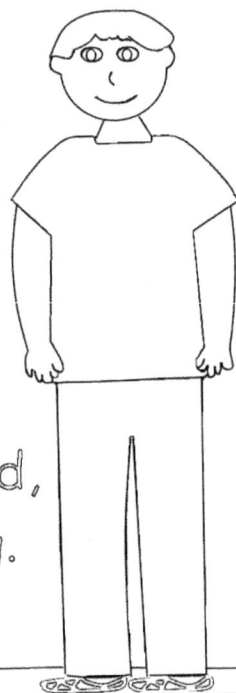

David

Sue

John

Mom

Dad

Sarah

Ann

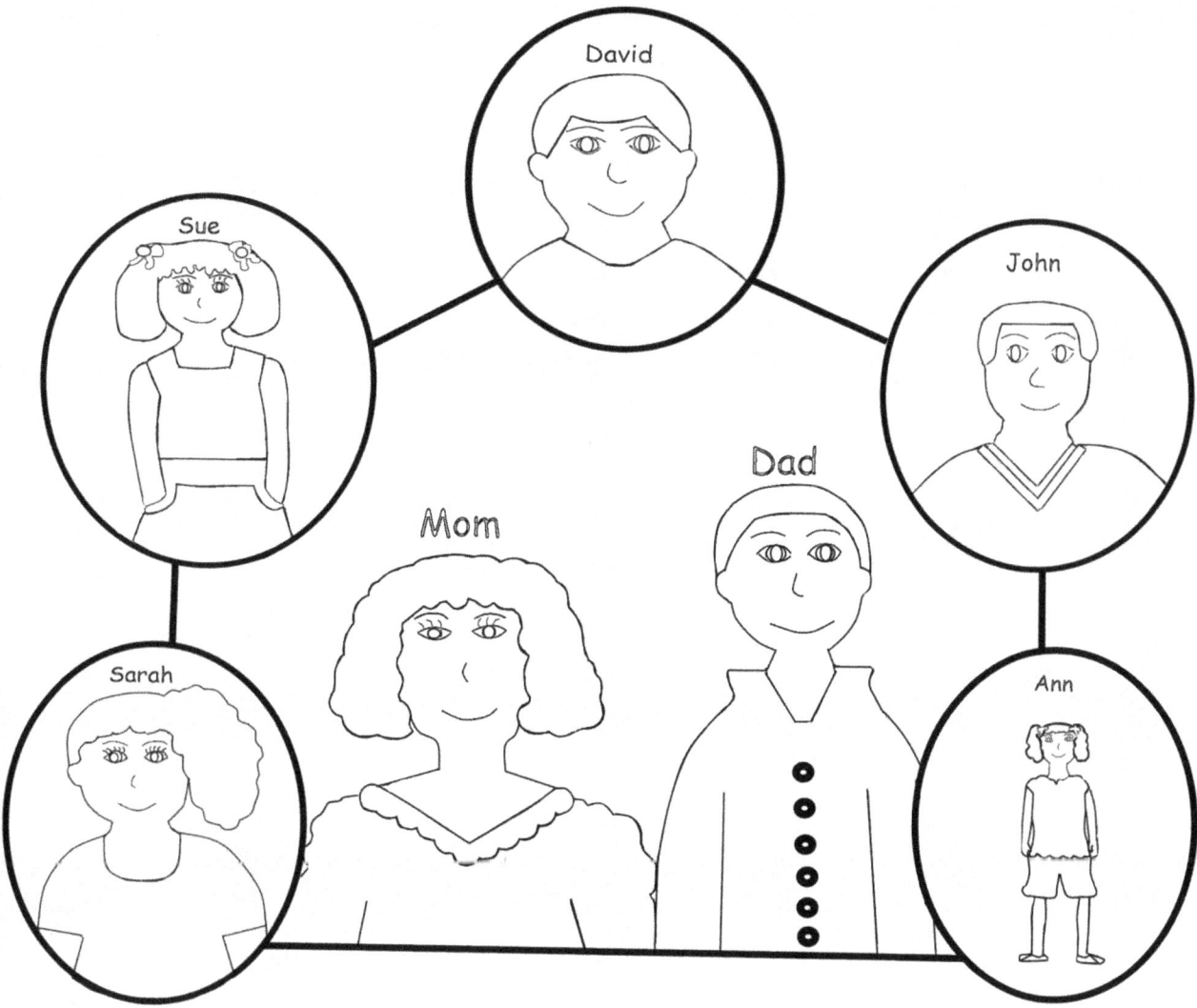

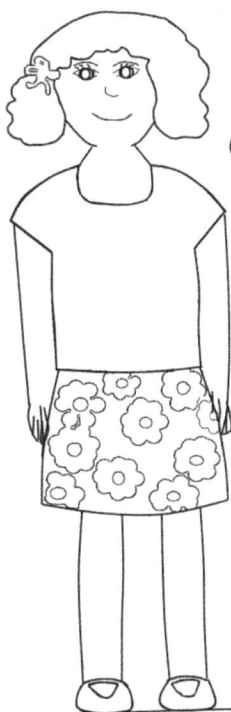

God told the man and woman to do good and to increase in number.

This is my family and it is still growing.

Instructions

Draw pictures of 4 family members in the circles below.

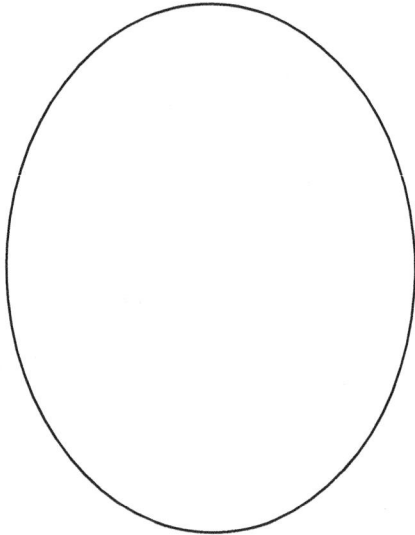

<u>Name</u>

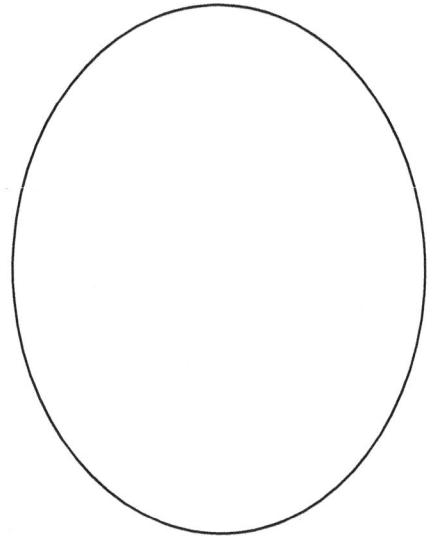

<u>Name</u>

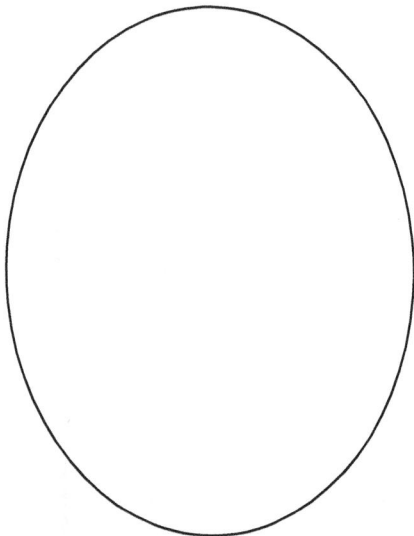

<u>Name</u>

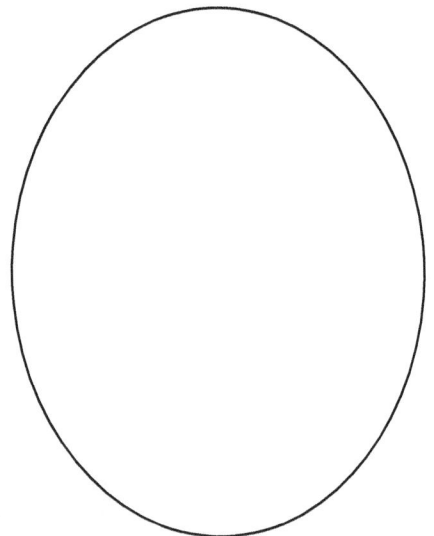

<u>Name</u>

On the 7th day, God rested from all of his hard work.

He was finished making the heavens and the earth and everything in it.

God made the 7th day holy and blessed all that he created.

The End

About the Author

Yolanda N. Brannon, Psy.D. is a Florida licensed psychologist who completed her doctoral degree in Clinical Psychology at the Florida Institute of Technology in Melbourne, FL. Prior to completing her doctoral studies, she obtained a Master of Science degree in Counseling and Clinical Health Psychology from the Philadelphia College of Osteopathic Medicine in Philadelphia, PA. Dr. Brannon is an alumna of South Carolina State University in Orangeburg, SC, where she completed a Bachelor of Science degree in Psychology. She also holds a Bachelor of Biblical Studies from Andersonville Theological Seminary located in Camilla, GA.   Dr. Brannon is also a Professor of Psychology, a bible-based teacher, author, and illustrator. She enjoys using her gift and love for writing to inspire others and to spread the "good news" of Jesus Christ around the world.

If this book has encouraged you in any way,
this author would love to hear from you.

She is also available for speaking engagements.
You may contact her at:

Manna Expressions, LLC
PO Box 26971
Fayetteville, NC 28314

or

Toll free at (888) 978-4246
or at the following email address:
mannaexpressions@aol.com

Christian Children's Author & Illustrator

Yolanda N. Brannon

Look for these book titles

Jesus Loves Always

Jesus Loves Always Coloring Book

Jesus Loves Always Activity Book

God Made Me, the Earth, and the Sea

God Made Me, the Earth, and the Sea Coloring and Activity Book

Manna Expressions, LLC

mannaexpressions.com

www.ingramcontent.com/pod-product-compliance
Lightning Source LLC
Chambersburg PA
CBHW081233020426
42331CB00012B/3150